No part of this work may be reproduced, incorporated into a computer system, or transmitted in any form or by any means (electronic, mechanical, photocopying, recording or otherwise) without the prior written permission of the copyright holders. Infringement of such rights may constitute an intellectual property crime.

ISBN: 978-91-89848-82-5

40 Things I Want to Do with You Forever © Grete Books, 2025

THIS IS A GIFT

FROM:

TO:

DATE:

HAVE BREAKFAST IN BED

GO FOR A BIKE RIDE TOGETHER IN THE MORNING

WATCH A SUNRISE TOGETHER

GO TO THE **DRIVE-IN** AND WATCH A MOVIE IN THE CAR UNDER THE OPEN SKY

GO CAMPING UNDER THE STARS

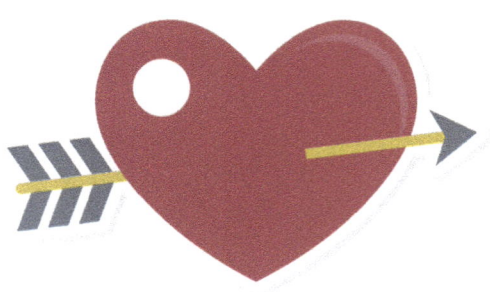

TAKE DANCE CLASSES TOGETHER AND LEARN TO DANCE AS A COUPLE

KISS EVERY PART OF YOUR BODY

SURPRISE EACH OTHER WITH A SPECIAL **DINNER** WITHOUT WARNING

EXPLORE AN UNFAMILIAR NEIGHBORHOOD IN OUR CITY TOGETHER

What would your ideal vacation together be?

_____
_____
_____
_____
_____

GO ON A DATE **DRESSED AS CHARACTERS** COMPLETELY DIFFERENT FROM OURSELVES

SPEND A DAY IN THE COUNTRYSIDE AND ESCAPE THE CITY

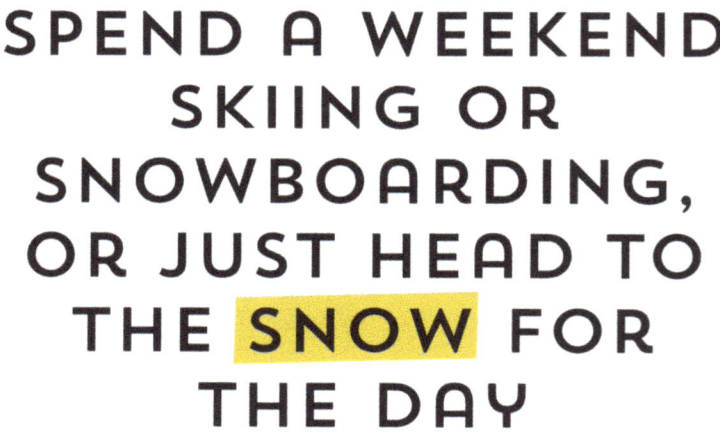

SPEND A WEEKEND SKIING OR SNOWBOARDING, OR JUST HEAD TO THE SNOW FOR THE DAY

LISTEN TO OUR FAVORITE RECORDS TOGETHER

RENT A CLASSIC **CONVERTIBLE** AND GO ON A ROAD **TRIP**

Is there a song that reminds you of me whenever you hear it?

SING TOGETHER AT THE TOP OF OUR LUNGS, EVEN IF WE'RE OFF-KEY

GO PARTYING
AND COME BACK AT THE CRACK OF DAWN

SHARE OUR UNSPOKEN ROMANTIC **FANTASIES** AND MAKE ONE (OR ALL!) COME TRUE.

LIE ON THE GRASS, GAZE AT THE STARS, AND SHARE A BOTTLE OF WINE AND A MEANINGFUL CONVERSATION

ENJOY A NIGHT OF BOARD OR CARDS GAMES

PRACTICE A SONG EACH TO PERFORM AND SING IT FOR EACH OTHER

GO TO A BOOKSTORE AND PICK A BOOK FOR YOU, AND HAVE YOU PICK A BOOK FOR ME

SHARE A BUBBLE BATH WITH CANDLES

THROW A PARTY AT HOME FOR TWO, WITH MUSIC AND DANCING

GAZE INTO EACH OTHER'S EYES IN SILENCE

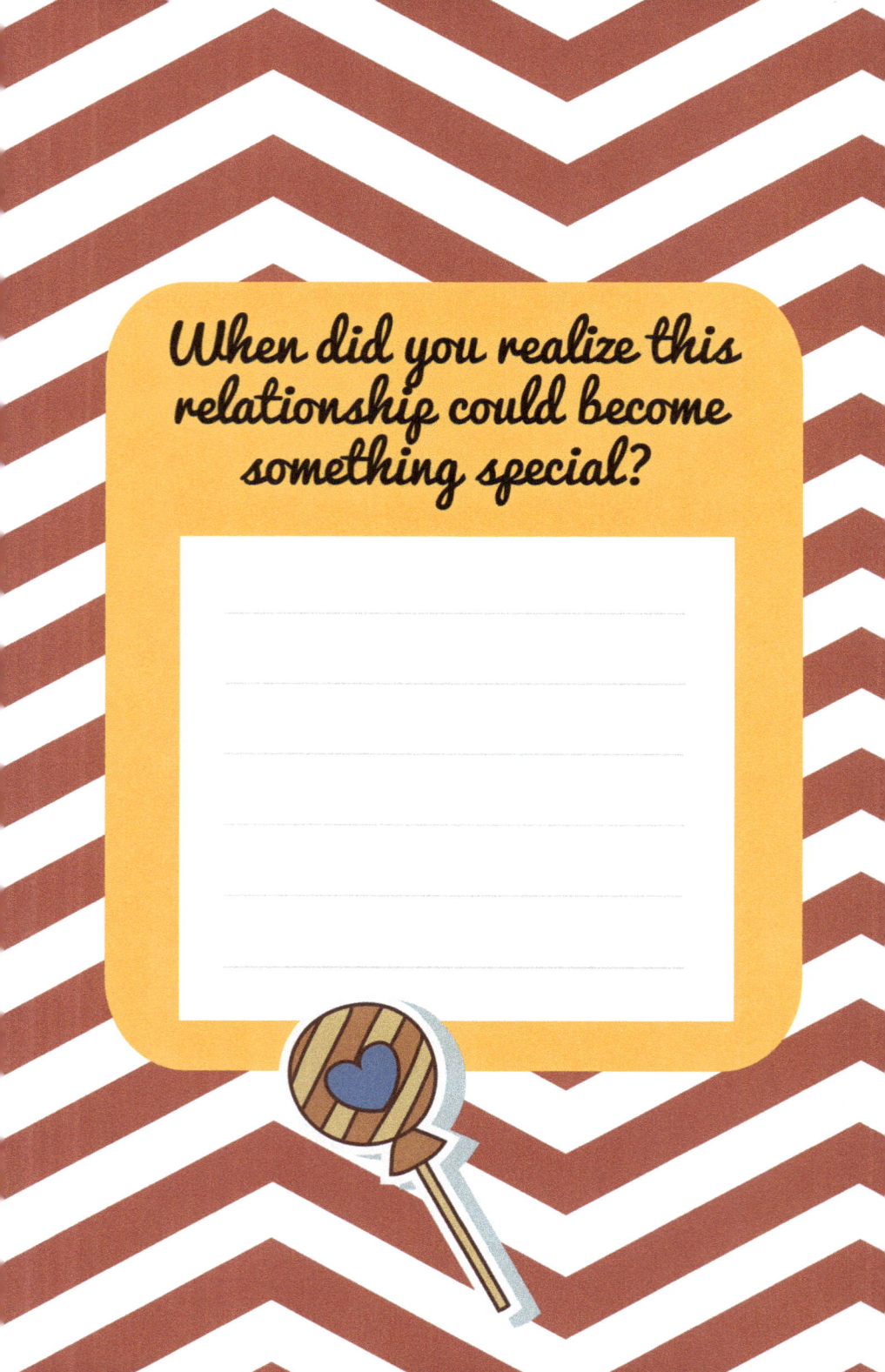

When did you realize this relationship could become something special?

READ THE SAME **BOOK** AT THE SAME TIME

STROLL HAND IN HAND AROUND THE CITY

HAVE A MOVIE MARATHON WITH POPCORN AT HOME

SET UP A
PICNIC AND
SAVOR A WARM
SUMMER
AFTERNOON
TOGETHER

LEARN TO COOK A DISH THAT WE BOTH LOVE

GO TO THE **THEATER** OR SEE THAT MUSICAL WE'VE ALWAYS DREAMED OF ATTENDING.

If you could travel back in time, which moment would you choose to relive with me?

TRY A
NEW RESTAURANT
IN THE CITY

DRAW A PORTRAIT OF EACH OTHER IN PENCIL, OIL, WATERCOLOR... AND FRAME THEM, NO MATTER HOW THEY TURN OUT!

REMEMBER HOW WE MET AND **RELIVE** THAT TIME BY VISITING THE PLACES WHERE WE HAD OUR FIRST DATES

What's the best memory you have of me so far?

_____
_____
_____
_____
_____

HAVE A
PHOTO SESSION
WITH EACH OTHER
AND PRINT OUT
THE BEST SHOTS

SPEND A DAY PLANNING THE **TRIPS** WE DREAM OF TAKING TOGETHER

HAVE AN AFTERNOON AT THE BOWLING ALLEY

EXPLORE OUR OWN CITY AS TOURISTS AND DISCOVER MUSEUMS WITH PAINTINGS AND SCULPTURES WE'VE NEVER SEEN

WRITE A POEM FOR EACH OTHER AND READ IT ALOUD

WEAR MATCHING OUTFITS FOR A DAY